the
other
city

The Other City
derives from a school photography project
supported by a grant
from the Eastman Kodak Company,
which was administered by
the Horace Mann-Lincoln Institute
of School Experimentation at Teachers College,
Columbia University.

the other city

by Ray Vogel

with photographs and commentary by
William Boyd, James Freeman,
Alfonso Garcia and Ronald McCoy

David White, New York

Library of Congress Catalog Card Number: 69-18087

Published by David White, Inc.
60 East 55th Street
New York, New York 10022

Book and jacket design by Arnold Skolnick

Printed by Rapoport Printing, New York

How this book came about
by
Ray Vogel

A teacher in the New York City School System

My school is in the heart of a ghetto area. It was a great day when we were presented with a lively challenge—the opportunity to bypass established curriculum in order to offer students with a limited academic background a new means of creative expression and communication. We were to become part of an experimental photography project and nine boys from the seventh grade were chosen to participate. They were given their own Instamatic cameras, as much school time as they needed, as well as free transportation.

As was natural, the boys started with what they knew best, and they began to photograph their immediate surroundings —boarded-up abandoned houses, wrecked cars, garbage-filled lots, and decrepit tenements. They then turned to pictures of themselves, usually acting out some tough guy role for the lens.

The resulting photographs were naturals for follow-up classroom study and discussion. Those depicting so poignantly the rot in their community were provocative enough to induce usually uncommunicative boys to enter into a discussion of the conditions they had themselves revealed, and then write about what could be done to remedy these ills. By vocalizing these problems, the boys gained some understanding of both their rights and responsibilities as citizens. Many who had never before attempted to put things down in writing began putting into words their ideas about community change—and even city planning.

When the school year ended, four of the boys continued taking pictures for this book. Although they had taken hundreds of photographs during the regular school year, these four enthusiastic youngsters took several hundred additional pictures from which the final selections were made. The substance of the text was taken from a tape recording session with the boys and from their own written material. The photographs are very much their own—they have neither been cropped nor retouched in any way.

Hopefully, *The Other City* will give young people who lead more comfortable lives a better understanding of the conditions in which many less-fortunate people live. It dramatically and realistically portrays the life style of the ghetto as it tells it like it is: what it's like to be a boy growing up in one of America's many *other cities*.

the
other
city

I took this picture from a fire escape. I think that's the Empire State Building over there.

*Around where I live
the houses are beat-up
and the streets are dirty.*

Garbage, garbage, garbage, garbage…

You can always see clotheslines stretched across backyards.

Around my block you see a lot of burned-
out cars just lying in the street. People
rob the car and sell the pieces. Then they
burn it so the cops can't find fingerprints.
I saw two little kids burn a car once. They
just lit up the cushion.

Nobody lives in these beat-up buildings because they don't have windows or heat.

People around here use buses and subways to get to work or school.

*People throw things in the empty lots. They're not supposed to
and if they get caught they pay a fine. But they never get caught.*

*You can be walking along and see empty lots that could be
fixed up for a playground or a park. Maybe somebody should
plant some trees. But they don't.*

There was a big fire.
Fourteen people died.
Nine children.
People demonstrate and carry signs
about how they want a better place to live.

people

Kids have fun hanging around together.
There are lots of kids your own age to play with.

You can always find somebody to be your friend.

*You can sit on a stoop
and eat watermelon…*

Or you can play in front of a store.

Sometimes there's nothing to do except sit around.

In summer we go to the recreation center.

*When it gets real hot inside, your mother lets you play
on the fire escape. A lot of kids play on fire escapes.
I play on the roof.*

When you grow up, you get tired of a lot of the street games. They don't seem as much fun as they used to.

Some kids quit school because they don't like it.
Or maybe they have to make money for their family.
This center helps kids go back to school.

Finding work around here is hard.

Seven, eight, or ten or twenty—I don't know how many people live here. Sometimes fifteen or sixteen people live in a four-room apartment.

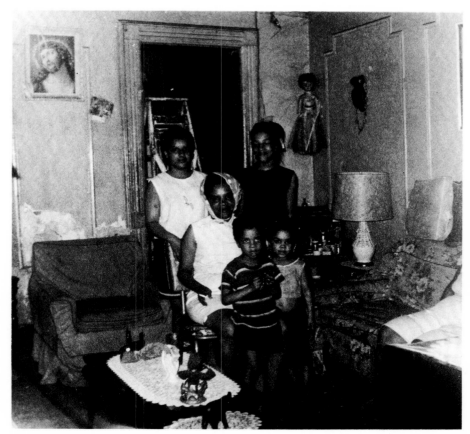

The landlord did a cheap job of painting and we had to go over it. He bought this kind of waterpaint.

school and fun

There are lots of games we play.
Girls always like to skip rope.

We play stickball.
If you hit the wall three windows high, it's a triple.
The strike's in a box in the middle of the wall.

You can play basketball with a fire escape ladder for
a hoop.

*If you have a bicycle you can ride
and go anywhere you want to.*

Some days you might just feel
like hitting around an old tin can with a stick.

*Sometimes we go to play centers
with a lot of other kids around our block.*

This is where I go to school. It's pretty beat up.

*Sometimes we like
to fool around in class.*

We play handball. The playgrounds have fences around them.

There aren't many trees around our block.
But if you see one, there's probably somebody climbing
in it. I like to take pictures of trees.

Most playgrounds have bars that kids swing on.

They wouldn't let us in to take pictures of this pool.
They thought we were trying to sneak in
so I climbed to the top of the fence and took this picture.
The pool gets real crowded when it's hot.

If you don't go to a pool
you can turn on a "johnny pump."

It's fun shooting the pump. If you use tin cans with both ends cut out, you can aim the water anywhere you want to. You can't use two cans though or you'll cut your hands. That water's strong.

When a building burns down,
it's just left there, all burned out.
Kids like to play around these lots.
It's dangerous but it's fun.

A lot of men play dominos
and pitch pennies.

shopping

Men push carts and sell fruit and vegetables.
We pick up fruit from them.
At school they give us welfare food—just cheese,
a big fat thick piece of cheese.

You can buy second-hand stuff
in stores like these.

You can buy good clothes from stores
that put their clothes out on the sidewalk.

Kids buy records and guitars here.
A lot of people can't read English
so you see signs in Spanish, too.

Your mother can pick out the kind of fish
she wants at the fish market.

jobs

You always want to make a little money.
You make a shoe shine box
and start your own business.

These men are loading up wood
from a house that burned down.
It's rough work but they pay good.

That's the coconut man.
He scrapes the coconut and puts
some canned milk in it, and sugar.
Then he puts ice in it.
It's cold and it's good.

The mailman has a good job
and makes a lot of money.
I wouldn't mind being a mailman.

The garbage truck picks up the garbage every Monday around my block. They should come more often because it piles up and stinks. Last year some people tried to burn their garbage and they put their own building on fire.

I wouldn't want to be a cop. People call them bulls, flatfeet, fuzz and pigs.

getting away

*Sometimes we go to Prospect Park
and eat outside at picnic tables.*

The zoo is a great place.
They've got all kinds of wild animals there in cages.

Sometimes we take the subway to Coney Island
to get a hot dog and go on the rides
like the Thunder Bolt and the Cyclone.

When the weather gets real hot,
we go to the beach to swim and cool off.

Some little kids wear their underwears at the beach.

I went on a ferryboat ride once.
I didn't want to come back.
I wanted to stay on the water.